Fighting Karate

J. Allen Queen

Sterling Publishing Co., Inc.   New York

To my wife, Patsy

Edited by Timothy Nolan

Photography by Samuel Jones, III

Diagrams by Patsy Queen

Original Artwork by John Huehnergarth

Library of Congress Cataloging-in-Publication Data
Queen, J. Allen.
  Fighting karate / by J. Allen Queen.
    p.   cm.
  Includes index.
  Summary: Discusses the skills, techniques, and exercises involved
in kumite, the art of freestyle karate sparring.
  ISBN 0-8069-6838-9
  1. Karate—Juvenile literature. [1. Karate.] I. Title.
GV1114.3.Q43 1989   88-22087
796.8'153—dc19   CIP
                                                     AC

1   3   5   7   9   10   8   6   4   2

Copyright © 1988 by J. Allen Queen
Published by Sterling Publishing Co., Inc.
Two Park Avenue, New York, N.Y. 10016
Distributed in Canada by Oak Tree Press Ltd.
% Canadian Manda Group, P.O. Box 920, Station U
Toronto, Ontario, Canada M8Z 5P9
Distributed in Great Britain and Europe by Cassell PLC
Artillery House, Artillery Row, London SW1P 1RT, England
Distributed in Australia by Capricorn Ltd.
P.O. Box 665, Lane Cove, NSW 2066
Manufactured in the United States of America
All rights reserved
Sterling ISBN 0-8069-6838-9

CONTENTS

Acknowledgments

I would like to thank the following students for their assistance, years of dedicated study with me, and cooperation, without which this book would not be possible: Antwaine Brown, Mallice Felder, Candace Graves, Jonathon Jones, Heather McDowell, Heidi McLeod, Holly McLeod, Kim Moore, Scott Myers, Travis Queen, Lesley Stitt, Max Washington, Ranata Wingo, Robert Wingo, Robert Wingo, Jr., and Steven Wood.

1

TOURNAMENT FIGHTING

Action! That is what you will find in karate. People your age are learning this
exciting sport, and you can too. With
practice and dedication you can kick and
punch with the fast action you see here.

Tournaments

Karate is a fighting art. It can be used as
a self-defense, and you can learn to protect yourself from an attacker. However,
the real fun and excitement is in sport
karate. Each year there are thousands of
tournaments where boys and girls like
you enter to win trophies and prizes.

Kumite (koo-ma-ta), or sparring, is the
most exciting event you can enter at a
tournament, but you do not have to
enter a tournament in order to kumite.
You can kumite with a friend in a gym,
garage, or any open space.

Illus. 1 (above) and Illus. 2 (below). In kumite, you use kicks and punches to score
points and win.

Illus. 3. Judges watch the kumite matches closely and decide who wins.

Illus. 4. These karate students are waiting to begin a kumite match.

Illus. 5. This boy shows the excitement in winning a karate trophy.

Tournament Rules & Equipment

Illus. 6. When you enter a tournament you must have a karate suit. A karate suit is called a *gi* (gee).

You can learn and practise karate in any loose clothing, and inexpensive suits can be purchased from some sporting goods shops. You can also order a suit from advertisements in karate magazines.

Illus. 7. Hand and foot gloves are required for protection in most tournaments.

Illus. 8. You can also wear additional equipment to protect your hands and legs.

Illus. 9. Kumite opponents are matched by rank, size, and, usually, age.

Illus. 10.

Illus. 11.

Illus. 12.

Illus. 10–12. You can score points in ku-mite by striking your opponent near the face, chest, or stomach area.

In many tournaments, especially at the lower ranks, you *do not* make actual contact. Learn to come within one or two inches of the target areas, and as you practise and learn with a friend, *never* make contact.

Illus. 13.

Illus. 14.

Illus. 15.

Illus. 13–15. Additional targets are the groin, the neck, or the side of the head.

You score a point when a kick or punch is not blocked. If it is blocked, no point is awarded.

In most tournaments, the first person to score three points wins the match.

Winners continue in kumite until the final four undefeated fighters are determined. The two pairs fight, and if you are one of the two winners, you spar for first or second place. If you win the final match you win first place—and get the largest prize.

Infractions

When sparring you must be careful not to break the rules or make an infraction.

An infraction can occur if you strike your opponent too low, usually below the groin level, go out of the ring or are unsportsmanlike or disrespectful. Striking or charging at your opponent could also be an infraction. If you are charged with an infraction of a rule, you could receive a warning, lose a point or be disqualified. It depends upon whether or not the infraction is repeated or anger was shown. Remember—be extra careful and always be a good sportsman.

Illus. 17. You could be disqualified if you commit an infraction.

Illus. 16. If a judge raises his hand in a circular manner, this means a rule has been broken.

Illus. 18. In most kumite matches, there is a center judge and two corner judges. As the match begins, you bow, to show respect, to the center judge and then to your opponent.

Illus. 19. Bow; then get into your fighting stance (You will learn this in Chapter 3).

Illus. 20. Once the referee starts the match, you are free to strike.

Illus. 21. The center judge will signal when you receive a point . . .

Illus. 22. . . . and when no point is awarded.

Illus. 23. Unfortunately, you sometimes may strike successfully but the judges did not see the point.

Illus. 24. If he gives this signal, it means he did not see the point. Always try to stand where the judges can see you.

Illus. 25. Always let the judges work out any problem without arguing.

In case of a tie, the match continues until the first point is scored. It is important never to argue with judges about their decisions. Let the judges and tournament officials work out the problem. Always respect their decision.

Do your best. Tournament fighting is rough. Kicks are hard and the speed is fast, but with the right preparation you will succeed. Be careful and good luck.

2
TRAINING EXERCISES

FLEXIBILITY EXERCISES

Two things you will need to kumite are flexibility and speed. Flexibility will let you kick higher with less effort and speed will let you punch and kick faster.

Do the following exercises daily as a warm-up before karate practice so you can practise safely. It's also a good idea to *slowly* do these exercises after your workout, as a cool-down activity.

It's important to remember not to stretch too hard. *Don't force yourself* if it becomes painful. With time and practice you'll have no trouble at all.

Neck Roll

Illus. 26 (above left). Stand with your feet together and place your hands in front of you. Push your neck forward.

Illus. 27 (left). Move your head to your left slowly and stretch for a second.

Illus. 28 (above). Rotate your neck in a circle towards the back and back around to the front. Repeat five times.

Arm Rotations

This exercise will loosen up your shoulders. Do it ten times with each arm.

Illus. 29 (above left). Stand straight with your arms by your side. Begin raising your arm forward without bending your elbow.

Illus. 30 (left). Keep your arm straight and reach for the sky.

Illus. 31 (above). Continue rotating your arm behind you until your arm makes a full circle. Imagine you're winding up a clock or preparing to throw a baseball.

Leg Bends

Now warm up the muscles on the inside of your legs.

Illus. 32 (left). Stand with your left leg in front of you and your right leg slightly bent.

Illus. 33 (right). Slowly drop your right knee and begin to lower your weight onto it. Lock (do not bend) your left knee and stretch. You may have to hold your weight with your hands in the beginning. Repeat five times to the left and five times to the right.

Leg Split

This exercise will make you flexible.

Illus. 34 (left). Stand with your feet wide apart, knees bent. Slowly turn your left foot and move it forward. Keep your back leg straight.

Illus. 35 (right). Carefully stretch until you can't go any further. You can use your hands for support. Remember not to stretch too hard, and be careful! Repeat twice from the left and twice from the right.

Body Bends

This exercise will stretch your stomach, hips, and legs.

Illus. 36 (left). Begin by spreading your legs wide with your arms and hands straight up.

Illus. 37 (below left). Slowly bend your body forward, keeping your legs straight, and try to touch the floor. Don't get discouraged if you can't reach it. Just go as far as you can and *don't force*. As you practise you will go a little further with each exercise. Slowly come back up to the original position. Repeat ten times.

Illus. 38 (below). Move your feet inward about a shoulder's-width apart.

Illus. 39 (below). Slowly bend forward as far as you can. You probably won't go as far as you did before, but don't worry. With practice, you will reach the floor easily. Repeat ten times.

Illus. 40 (right). Stand with feet together and hands in the air.

Illus. 41 (below right). Slowly lower your arms forward. Remember not to bend your knees. Repeat ten times.

Leg Stretch

Leg stretches will give you some extra flexibility.

Illus. 42. Sit with your left leg behind you and your right leg straight out in front of you.

Illus. 43. Bend forward with both hands and try to touch your right toes. Bend as far as you can, but be careful not to stretch until it becomes painful. Repeat ten times with each leg. Try harder with each stretch.

Leg Swing

Leg swings will add balance and flexibility.

Illus. 44 (left). Stand straight with feet together.

Illus. 45 (below left). Swing your right leg up to your waist and lower it. Increase the height of your swing with each repetition.

Illus. 46 (below). Eventually, you will be able to swing your leg above your head. Repeat five times for each leg.

Two-Man Pull

This exercise requires a partner.

Illus. 47. Sit with your legs as wide apart as possible, facing your partner. He or she grabs your arms and places his feet against your legs right above your knees.

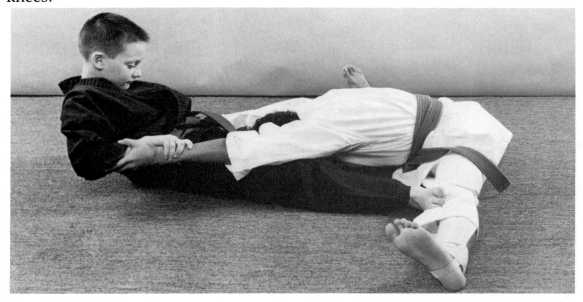

Illus. 48. Slowly bend over as your partner pulls you towards him. Stretch as far as possible without pain. Repeat three to five times.

Two-Man Lifts

This exercise also needs a partner.

Illus. 49. Stand on your left leg and raise your right leg into your partner's hands.

Illus. 50. On your command, your partner raises your leg as far as possible. Tell him when to stop. Remember, don't force! Repeat three to five times with each leg. Try standing against a wall if you need more balance.

SPEED EXERCISES

Power and speed will come with any exercise. However, there are a few you can do to work specifically on your speed.

Swinging Ball

Illus. 51 (above). As your partner holds and swings the ball to you, be ready to strike.

Illus. 52 (above right). Try to hit the ball with your fist as it comes to you.

Illus. 53 (right). Move fast to punch as your partner moves it higher and faster. Learn to focus on the target and try to figure the speed and hit the ball as it approaches. Practise for five minutes.

Moving Target

Illus. 54. Have your partner place his hands together and move them quickly as you try to punch them with your fist.

Illus. 55. Try to move faster as the target moves faster. Practise for five minutes. Your timing and speed will increase greatly as you practise.

Hand Slap

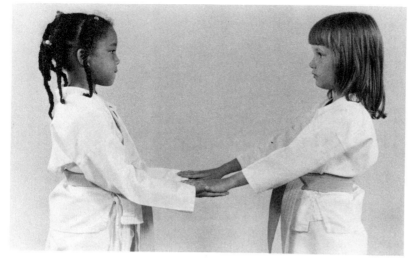

Illus. 56. Place the palms of your hands upwards under your partner's downwards palms. You want to *lightly* touch your partner's face with an open hand without being blocked.

Illus. 57. Quickly pull the left hand out.

Illus. 58. Swing fast and lightly tap your partner's face. Do the same with your other hand, and try to fake your partner by slightly moving your left hand and then quickly striking with the right. Do this for two to four minutes and don't forget to change places!

On Guard Slap

In this exercise, either person can strike at any time.

Illus. 59. Face your partner with your right arms touching each other, ready to strike. Your right feet should touch. Again, you want to *lightly* strike the face without getting blocked.

Illus. 60. Quickly move the hand under your opponent's.

Illus. 61. Extend and strike.

Speed Balance

Illus. 62 (below). On a straight line or a piece of tape, stand in a balancing position with arms out.

Illus. 63 (right). Bend over and run quickly on the line. As you reach the end of the tape or the line (about ten feet), stand up and quickly turn around on one foot.

Illus. 64 (below right). After you spin around, balance yourself and run quickly back to the starting position with your head and body straight. Repeat five times.

Fast Leg Swing

This exercise will help you gain leg speed. *Begin this exercise slowly* until you get very flexible.

Illus. 65. Stand with your right leg behind you and your hands near your chest.

Illus. 66. Bring your right leg past your left leg.

Illus. 67. Raise your leg to waist level, or as high as you can.

Illus. 68. Keep trying to lift your leg higher, but don't force. Be careful, and practise, practise, practise.

3
KUMITE SKILLS

The skills of blocking, striking, and kicking are the most important in kumite, as are the right stances and combinations.

KUMITE TECHNIQUES

Study the steps and photos carefully. Use the drawings to make sure your stances are correct.

Blocking

Use a *Front Stance* to defend with a *Rising Block*.

Illus. 69 (left). To execute these two moves: first bring your right leg in to your left; then prepare your block by crossing your left hand over your body.

Illus. 70 (below). From this starting position, take a step outward with your left foot while pulling up your left arm. Imagine you are moving forward to block a downwards strike on your head.

Illus. 71 (bottom). Complete the block by snapping your left arm upwards and pushing over half of your weight onto your front leg. Lock your back leg and rest your right hand on your right hip, ready to punch.

Illus. 72. Front stance.

In a similar fashion, do the *Lower Block* in a left front stance.

Illus. 73 (above left). From a ready position, pull your left arm up near your right shoulder.

Illus. 74 (left). At the same moment, begin to push outward with your left leg while turning your left arm downwards. Imagine you are blocking a kick to your lower abdomen.

Illus. 75 (above). Snap your arm into a full block, and, at the same time, fully extend your left foot. In the left front stance, slightly bend your front knee while keeping your back leg straight. Do the opposite to do the right front stance. Move your right leg in front and block with your right arm.

Move into the *Horse Stance* to do the *Center Blocks*. In the horse stance, simply pretend that you are riding a horse.

Illus. 76 (left). Spread both legs wide and bend your knees.

Illus. 77 (below left). To use an *Outside Center Block*, pull your right hand behind your right ear.

Illus. 78 (below). Slowly bring your right arm and hand around. Turn your arm completely in front of you, with the back of your hand facing upwards and the bottom heel of your hand ready for the block. Snap your arm back into position. Rest your left arm on your left hip, ready to punch.

Illus. 79. Horse stance.

43

Do an *Inside Center Block* from the horse stance.

Illus. 80 (left). Prepare your right hand by bringing it down and over your left leg.

Illus. 81 (below left). Now bring your arm up in a circle, so that you protect your side and stomach.

Illus. 82 (below). Snap your right arm into position by locking your arm. This time, the outside of your arm does the blocking. You can also use your left hand to do the center blocks, as well as any stance.

Throw the *Shuto Block*, or *Knife-Hand Block*, from a *Back Stance*.

Illus. 83 (below). Bend both knees slightly, your right leg a little deeper than your left, since it is holding more than half your weight. Keep your right hand against your chest. Pull your left hand back, palm inward.

Illus. 84 (right). Next, push your hand outward and turn the edge of your hand around to strike.

Illus. 85 (below right). Finish the block by fully extending your arm.

Illus. 86. Back stance.

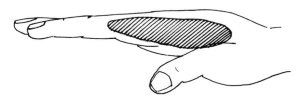

Illus. 87. Strike with the shaded area.

Punches

The *Karate Punch* is a strong striking weapon.

Illus. 89. Pull your right foot even with your left foot.

Illus. 88. Get into a left front stance. Pretend you have just landed a punch to the head with your left hand.

46

Illus. 91. Complete the punch with your right hand and be in a right front stance.

Illus. 90. Begin moving and rotating your right arm into a punching position as you keep moving your right leg forward.

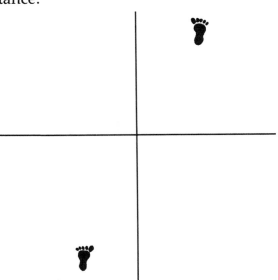

Illus. 92. Right front stance. To use this punch from the other side, just reverse the process.

Use the front stance for a *Ridge-Hand Strike*.

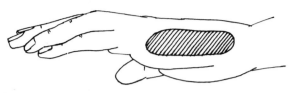

Illus. 93. The ridge of the hand with the thumb pulled back is the striking weapon.

Illus. 94 (below). Swing your right arm far behind you and keep it straight.

Illus. 95 (right). Continue the swing around with a driving force.

Illus. 96 (below right). Finish with your hand fully extended.

The *Back Fist* is a fast strike.

Illus. 97 (left). Get into a horse stance and place your right fist to your chest.

Illus. 98 (below left). Like a whip, snap the hand outward in a straight line.

Illus. 99 (below). As soon as the back of your hand strikes the target snap it back to the original position.

You probably know the *Shuto Strike* better as the "karate chop."

Illus. 100 (above). Get into a right back stance and place your right hand behind your head palm outward.

Illus. 101 (above right). Turn your upper body slightly and bring the knife edge of your hand around to strike.

Illus. 102 (right). As you make contact, snap your hand back to the original position. The strength of your shuto depends upon the snapping action of your arm and hand.

50

Kicks

Your legs are nearly three times as strong as your arms. Therefore, your kicks should be three times as strong as your punches. In karate, the three major kicks are the *Front Kick*, the *Side Kick*, and the *Roundhouse Kick*.

Illus. 103 (below). To throw the front kick, stand in a left front stance with both hands guarding your body.

Illus. 104 (right). Lift your right leg, bringing the knee towards your chest.

Illus. 105 (below right). Push the foot out, with your toes back, to kick. Strike with the ball of your foot. Keep your knee stiff and your toes back.

You can do a side kick from a horse stance.

Illus. 106. Bring your left leg up to your right knee level.

Illus. 107. Push your kick straight out as hard as you can. The heel and the outer edge of your foot are the striking areas. Try this kick with your right leg. As you become more flexible you will find yourself able to kick higher with each try.

The roundhouse kick will show you the results of your hard training when you see your speed increase.

Illus. 108 (below). Lift your right leg straight up from a front stance (as you did with a front kick). Drop your knee downwards and to your left. Keep your hand in front of you.

Illus. 109 (right). Snap your leg completely around to kick your opponent in the chest or head. The ball of your foot is the striking weapon.

Illus. 110 (below right). Snap the kick back immediately. Practise this kick with your left leg also.

COMBINING TECHNIQUES

To kumite well, you need to know the basic techniques, but you also need to know how to put them together. Try these situations with a partner to practise combining the techniques. Remember, though, not to make contact.

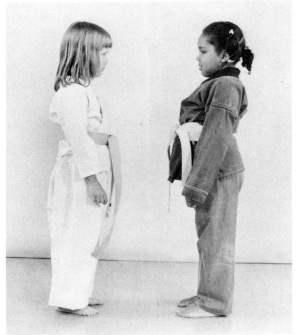

Situation One

Illus. 111 (left). Stand facing your opponent in a ready position.

Illus. 112 (below left). As he prepares to strike you in the head, step back into a right front stance and use a rising block.

Illus. 113 (below). Follow the block with a left punch to the chest.

Situation Two

Illus. 114. Face your opponent.

Illus. 115. As he moves to kick you, move into a lower block with a right front stance.

Illus. 116. As you move to punch . . .

Illus. 117. . . . he attempts a right punch to your head.

Illus. 118. Step back to block and prepare to set up a kick.

Illus. 119. Complete the front kick towards the groin or stomach area.

57

Situation Three

Illus. 120. Get into a ready position.

Illus. 121. Step into a left back stance to block your opponent's kick.

58

Illus. 122. Lift up your leg and deliver a right side kick to your opponent's stomach.

Illus. 123. Finish by throwing a right back fist to your opponent's head.

Situation Four

Illus. 124. As your opponent punches, **block** with an inside center block.

Illus. 125. Prepare to strike your opponent with a shuto or knife-hand strike.

Illus. 126. Strike your opponent with the shuto.

Situation Five

Illus. 127. Block your opponent's front kick with an outside center block. Step back and bring your arm around to complete the block.

Illus. 128. Strike your opponent with a back fist.

Illus. 129. Complete the series with a roundhouse kick to your opponent's chest area.

Illus. 130. Stand guard against your opponent.

Illus. 131. Use a left rising block to defend against a right punch.

Illus. 132. With your right hand deliver an immediate right punch to your opponent's chest area.

Illus. 133. Strike with a low side kick.

Illus. 134. Your opponent comes now with a right punch. Block with an inside center block.

Illus. 135. Spin by dropping your right leg behind your left leg.

64

Illus. 136. Continue spinning and prepare to strike with a right back fist.

Illus. 137. Complete the spin and strike with the back fist to the head.

Remember, you can step up or back into a front stance in preparing your defense. Judge your opponent's distance. Also, be sure to practise using blocks, kicks, and punches with both the left and right hands and feet.

4
FREESTYLE KUMITE

In kumite, you will face many different types of fighters. Offensive fighters are usually more aggressive in kumite. They go after the point instead of waiting for an opponent to charge. A defensive fighter stops the charge, and then scores. After trying both offensive and defensive fighting, see which one works better for you.

Whatever style you choose, you must develop a proper sparring stance—either a front stance, a back stance, or a horse stance.

Illus. 138. When in a sparring stance, always stand firm and keep your hands up to protect your body and head.

OFFENSIVE SPARRING

In offensive sparring you must learn how to move and deliver a strike. To do this, close the distance or gap between you and your opponent.

Illus. 139. As you begin your charge, step inside the opponent's area—step where he is standing.

Illus. 140. This makes it impossible for him to escape your charge, and you score with a front punch in a forward stance to the stomach.

Illus. 141. When you charge without entering your opponent's space, he easily moves out of the way and you do not score.

During sparring you should have on gloves and foot pads, but *don't hit!* Just come within two inches of the target and leave contact to the higher belts.

Situation 1

Here are a few offensive techniques.

Illus. 142. Get into a left front stance.

Illus. 143. Quickly fake a back fist to your opponent's head.

Illus. 144. As he raises his arm to block, score with a front kick to the stomach.

Situation 2

Illus. 145. This time use a horse stance.

Illus. 146. Again, throw a back fist to try to score.

Illus. 147. If you are blocked go to a left side kick.

Situation 3

Illus. 148. Using the round-house position, try to score with a punch to the chest.

Illus. 149. If your punch is blocked, move into position for a roundhouse kick by lifting your right leg.

Illus. 150. Extend the kick to the head for the score.

Situation 4

Illus. 151. Try to score with a left side kick. In this case you are blocked.

Illus. 152. Your opponent now charges you with a left punch.

Illus. 153. Block the punch and score with a left punch to the chest...

Illus. 154. ...a front kick to the stomach.

Try many ways to strike or kick. Use different stances to cover the distance. Be creative—but as always be careful.

DEFENSIVE SPARRING

Defensive fighters prefer to let their opponents move first; then block and try to score with a kick or punch. Timing is most important in being a good defensive fighter because you must block immediately after you see your opponent move; then strike faster than your opponent can block you. Try these techniques.

Situation 5

Illus. 155. Your oponent comes with a front punch to your head. You immediately block with a rising block.

Illus. 156. Score with a front kick to the stomach.

Situation 6

Illus. 157. You defend against a roundhouse kick with an outside center block. Keep your right hand in position to punch.

Illus. 158. Lunge forward with the punch to the head or chest. If the opponent is further back, step into the punch with a right front stance to close the distance.

Illus. 159. Use a back stance and lower block to defend a side kick.

Illus. 160. Immediately step in and strike your opponent's head with a back fist.

Illus. 161. Block a high right roundhouse kick to your head.

Illus. 162. Score with a right roundhouse to your opponent's chest or head.

Illus. 163. Stop your opponent's punch with a left inside center block.

Illus. 164. Deliver a front kick with your right leg to the opponent's stomach.

Illus. 165. If you miss or are blocked, set your foot down and move forward with a back fist strike.

Situation 10

Illus. 166. Fall back and stop your opponent's front kick with a lower block.

Illus. 167. Pick up your left leg and strike out with a left side kick to your opponent's stomach.

Situation 11

Illus. 168. Block a right punch to your head.

86

Illus. 169. As you counter with a front kick, your opponent moves back and blocks.

Illus. 170. When this happens, lift your knee and deliver a super-fast roundhouse kick to your opponent's head.

Situation 12

Illus. 171. Get into your sparring stance.

Illus. 172. As he throws a roundhouse, stop the score with an outside center block.

Illus. 173. As your opponent's foot comes down, fire a right roundhouse kick to his head.

Situation 13

Illus. 174. Get into your stance.

Illus. 175. Your opponent kicks. Block with a left lower block from a back stance position.

Illus. 176. You try to score with a punch, but you are too far away and your opponent blocks it easily.

Illus. 177. Your opponent attempts to punch low. Block.

Illus. 178. Deliver a left side kick to the stomach for the score.

FIGHTING DIFFERENT OPPONENTS

Illus. 179. Some fighters are called "chargers" because they often leap towards their opponents to score.

Illus. 180. To counter this type of fighter move out to your side and block.

Illus. 181. Then return a punch to his chest.

Illus. 182. A "bull" does not move when he is charged.

Illus. 183. The bull simply uses strength and speed to block the opponent.

94

Illus. 184. Many times he matches strike per strike with his opponent. The bull is usually slower, so he waits until there is a clear opening before striking.

Illus. 185. Sometimes you may experience the "bouncer," who moves or bounces up and down and from side to side.

Illus. 186. As he moves, conserve your energy and watch his movement.

Illus. 187. Just as he begins to get into a fighting stance, charge with a left punch to the chest.

Illus. 188. If this is blocked, move quickly and deliver a right punch to your opponent's head.

SCORING SECRETS

Being a good fighter is most important in kumite, but knowing a few scoring secrets might give you an even better chance against your opponent.

Illus. 189. As you already know, a good stance is important.

Illus. 190. By learning to be right on top of your opponent in closing a gap, you catch him off guard and defenseless.

An additional skill is faking ability. If you can get your opponent to block a fake move, he leaves himself wide open for attack.

Illus. 191. From a horse stance fighting position, try a fake.

Illus. 192. Move in as though you were going to deliver a back fist.

Illus. 193. Your opponent commits more by attempting to block.

Illus. 194. Lift your leg and deliver a roundhouse kick to his head.

Know where the judges are.

Illus. 195.

Illus. 195–196. Sometimes you may score with a punch or kick, but the judges are unable to see your punch or strike.

Illus. 196.

Illus. 197. Try to make sure the judges are in direct view when you deliver a punch or kick.

Develop your own style. Know your strengths.

Illus. 198. You may have a super fast roundhouse kick.

Illus. 199. You also may develop a powerful side kick.

Know your distance.

Illus. 200.

Illus. 200–201. A few inches may mean the difference between a score or no score.

Illus. 201.

Learn your weaknesses.

Illus. 202–203. Dropping your head or leaning forward can make you an easy target.

Illus. 203.

Dedication and practice will eliminate your weaknesses.

5

SELF-DEFENSE

Most of the kumite you do will be in tournaments. However, you may sometime find yourself in a situation where you will need to defend yourself with your karate skills. Hopefully, you will never need to use your karate skills against a real attack, but it is important to be prepared. Remember, though, when you practise to *never make actual contact*.

GRABS AND BREAKS

With two attackers you may find that being able to grab and break your attacker's hold will be your best defense.

Situation One

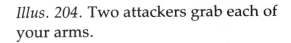

Illus. 204. Two attackers grab each of your arms.

Illus. 205. Lift up your right leg and kick the first attacker with a side kick. Remember to use the heel and knife edge of your foot.

Illus. 206. Lift up the arms of your other attacker.

Illus. 207. Deliver a front kick to his stomach or chest.

Situation Two

Illus. 208. Someone grabs you from behind and chokes you. As a second attacker approaches, deliver a driving front kick to his stomach.

Illus. 209. Grab your other attacker's wrist with your left hand. Grab his arm above the elbow with your right hand.

Illus. 210. Step out with your right leg and bend downwards and towards your attacker.

Illus. 211. Continue to turn and pull out from your attacker's grip. Keep holding his arm. Your right arm is up and ready to strike down to break his arm.

Illus. 212. Bring your right arm down like a hammer on the arm.

Illus. 213. Finish the move with a front kick to your attacker's chest.

ESCAPE TECHNIQUES

Escape techniques can get you out of a dangerous situation having many attackers.

Situation Three

Illus. 214. Two attackers grab your arms and a third begins to choke you.

Illus. 215. Immediately, kick the individual in front of you in the stomach or groin.

Illus. 216. Set your foot back down; then lift and throw a right side kick to the attacker on your right.

Illus. 217. Now turn and kick your last attacker in the groin area.

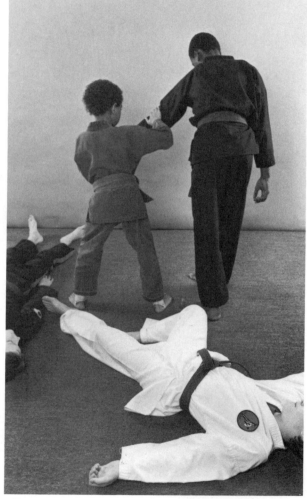

Illus. 218. As he bends over from pain, turn and grab him by the arm with both of your arms.

Illus. 219. Force him to the ground.

Illus. 220. Turn and escape.

Remember, when you practise, *do not hit*. You would only hurt someone if they were attacking you and trying to seriously hurt you.

119

Situation Four

Illus. 221. Three attackers surround you.

Illus. 222. The first attacker throws a punch. Block with a left upwards block.

Illus. 223. Now grab his arm with your left hand and wrap your right arm around it. Snap your right arm towards you, breaking his arm.

Illus. 224. Throw your elbow into the right side of his head.

Illus. 225. As the second attacker steps in to you, jump into his space with a right side kick.

Illus. 226. Face your last attacker, and use your kumite moves to put him down.

As you finish this book you will know the basics of karate. Karate, of course, can be used as self-defense, but its benefits go far beyond that. Exercise and discipline from practising karate will keep your body and your mind in shape. Your self-confidence will also grow as you enter and win tournaments.

To move up in karate rankings you will have to find a qualified instructor who can take you from the intermediate level to the advanced level. Information and guidelines about qualified instructors can be found by contacting the International Children's Karate Association (ICKA) in Raleigh, North Carolina.

Remember to practise and work hard, and you'll soon see the results. Above all, have fun.

INDEX